Chinese New Year

Julie Murray

Abdo Kids Junior
is an Imprint of Abdo Kids
abdobooks.com

Abdo
HOLIDAYS
Kids

abdobooks.com

Published by Abdo Kids, a division of ABDO, P.O. Box 398166, Minneapolis, Minnesota 55439.
Copyright © 2019 by Abdo Consulting Group, Inc. International copyrights reserved in all countries.
No part of this book may be reproduced in any form without written permission from the publisher.
Abdo Kids Junior™ is a trademark and logo of Abdo Kids.

Printed in the United States of America, North Mankato, Minnesota.

102018

012019

 THIS BOOK CONTAINS
RECYCLED MATERIALS

Photo Credits: Alamy, AP Images, Getty Images, iStock, Shutterstock

Production Contributors: Teddy Borth, Jennie Forsberg, Grace Hansen

Design Contributors: Christina Doffing, Candice Keimig, Dorothy Toth

Library of Congress Control Number: 2018946178

Publisher's Cataloging-in-Publication Data

Names: Murray, Julie, author.

Title: Chinese New Year / by Julie Murray.

Description: Minneapolis, Minnesota : Abdo Kids, 2019 | Series: Holidays set 2 |
    Includes glossary, index and online resources (page 24).

Identifiers: ISBN 9781532181702 (lib. bdg.) | ISBN 9781532182686 (ebook) |
    ISBN 9781532183171 (Read-to-me ebook)

Subjects: LCSH: Chinese New Year--Juvenile literature. | Holidays, festivals, &
    celebrations--Juvenile literature. | China--Social life and customs--Juvenile
    literature. | Ethnic festivals--Juvenile literature.

Classification: DDC 394.2614--dc23

Table of Contents

Chinese New Year 4

Signs of
Chinese New Year 22

Glossary 23

Index 24

Abdo Kids Code 24

Chinese New Year

Chinese New Year is here!

It lasts for 15 days.

It is in January or February.

Chun gets ready.

She cleans her home.

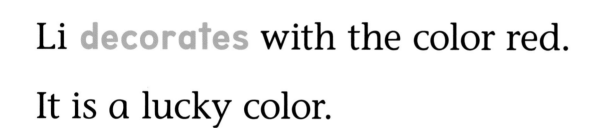

Li **decorates** with the color red.

It is a lucky color.

Amy hangs up lucky sayings.

Jin watches a lion dance.

Lions are good luck!

Ya has a meal with
her family.

Mia opens a gift. It is a red envelope. It has money inside.

It is the **Lantern Festival**. Ling hangs a lantern. They light up the night!

Signs of Chinese New Year

dragons

lanterns

lucky sayings

red envelopes

Glossary

decorate
to make more beautiful by adding decorations or designs.

Lantern Festival
a Chinese festival marking the final day of Chinese New Year celebrations.

lion dance
a traditional Chinese dance performed on big occasions for good luck.

Index

décor 10, 12, 20

gifts 18

Lantern Festival 20

length 4

lion dance 14

meal 16

month 6

preparations 8

symbols 10, 14

Abdo Kids
ONLINE
FREE! ONLINE MULTIMEDIA RESOURCES

Visit **abdokids.com** and use this code to access crafts, games, videos, and more!

Abdo Kids Code:
HCK1702